50 Premium Dessert Dishes for Home

By: Kelly Johnson

Table of Contents

- Classic Tiramisu
- Molten Lava Chocolate Cake
- Crème Brûlée
- New York Cheesecake
- French Macarons
- Chocolate Soufflé
- Raspberry Almond Tart
- Baked Alaska
- Matcha Green Tea Cheesecake
- Churros with Chocolate Dipping Sauce
- Sticky Toffee Pudding
- Pistachio Baklava
- Vanilla Panna Cotta with Berry Compote
- Chocolate Eclairs
- Lemon Meringue Pie
- Salted Caramel Brownies
- Almond Flour Chocolate Chip Cookies
- Opera Cake
- Flourless Chocolate Torte
- Tres Leches Cake
- Pumpkin Spice Roll Cake
- Pear and Almond Galette
- Red Velvet Cupcakes with Cream Cheese Frosting
- Black Forest Cake
- Strawberry Shortcake
- Carrot Cake with Walnuts
- Coconut Cream Pie
- Apple Strudel
- Classic Profiteroles
- Chocolate-Covered Strawberries
- Peanut Butter Mousse Cups
- White Chocolate Raspberry Blondies
- Mocha Tiramisu
- Passion Fruit Tart
- Japanese Cotton Cheesecake

- Chocolate-Dipped Biscotti
- Mango Sticky Rice
- Homemade Baklava
- Hazelnut Praline Cake
- Dulce de Leche Flan
- Matcha Swiss Roll
- Honey Lavender Ice Cream
- Chocolate Hazelnut Crepes
- Italian Cannoli
- Banana Foster
- Pecan Pie Bars
- Chocolate Espresso Mousse
- Rose Water Pistachio Cake
- Bourbon Bread Pudding
- Homemade S'mores

Classic Tiramisu

Ingredients:

- 3 egg yolks
- 1/2 cup granulated sugar
- 8 oz mascarpone cheese
- 1 cup heavy whipping cream
- 1 cup strong brewed espresso, cooled
- 2 tbsp coffee liqueur (optional)
- 24 ladyfinger biscuits
- Cocoa powder for dusting

Instructions:

1. In a bowl, whisk egg yolks and sugar until pale and creamy.
2. Add mascarpone cheese and mix until smooth.
3. In another bowl, whip heavy cream until stiff peaks form, then fold into the mascarpone mixture.
4. Mix espresso and coffee liqueur in a shallow dish.
5. Dip ladyfingers briefly into the coffee mixture and layer them in a dish.
6. Spread half of the mascarpone mixture over the ladyfingers.
7. Repeat with another layer of soaked ladyfingers and mascarpone.
8. Refrigerate for at least 4 hours or overnight.
9. Dust with cocoa powder before serving.

Molten Lava Chocolate Cake

Ingredients:

- 4 oz dark chocolate, chopped
- 1/2 cup unsalted butter
- 1/4 cup all-purpose flour
- 1/2 cup powdered sugar
- 2 eggs
- 2 egg yolks
- 1/2 tsp vanilla extract

Instructions:

1. Preheat oven to 425°F (220°C). Grease ramekins.
2. Melt butter and chocolate together, stirring until smooth.
3. In a bowl, whisk eggs, egg yolks, and sugar until thick.
4. Fold in melted chocolate mixture and vanilla.
5. Add flour and mix until just combined.
6. Divide batter between ramekins and bake for 12 minutes.
7. Let cool for 1 minute, then invert onto plates and serve warm.

Crème Brûlée

Ingredients:

- 2 cups heavy cream
- 4 egg yolks
- 1/2 cup granulated sugar
- 1 tsp vanilla extract
- 2 tbsp sugar (for caramelizing)

Instructions:

1. Preheat oven to 325°F (160°C).
2. Heat heavy cream in a saucepan until hot but not boiling.
3. In a bowl, whisk egg yolks and sugar. Slowly add warm cream while whisking.
4. Stir in vanilla and pour into ramekins.
5. Place ramekins in a baking dish with hot water halfway up the sides.
6. Bake for 35-40 minutes until set but slightly jiggly.
7. Cool completely, then refrigerate for at least 4 hours.
8. Sprinkle sugar on top and caramelize with a torch before serving.

New York Cheesecake

Ingredients:

- 2 cups graham cracker crumbs
- 1/2 cup melted butter
- 24 oz cream cheese, softened
- 1 cup sugar
- 3 eggs
- 1 tsp vanilla extract
- 1 cup sour cream

Instructions:

1. Preheat oven to 325°F (160°C).
2. Mix graham cracker crumbs and melted butter, then press into a springform pan.
3. Beat cream cheese and sugar until smooth. Add eggs one at a time.
4. Mix in vanilla and sour cream.
5. Pour batter over crust and bake for 50-55 minutes.
6. Cool completely, then refrigerate overnight before serving.

French Macarons

Ingredients:

- 1 cup almond flour
- 1 3/4 cups powdered sugar
- 3 egg whites
- 1/4 cup granulated sugar
- Food coloring (optional)

Instructions:

1. Sift almond flour and powdered sugar together.
2. Beat egg whites until foamy, then add granulated sugar and whip until stiff peaks form.
3. Fold in almond flour mixture gently.
4. Pipe rounds onto a baking sheet and let sit for 30 minutes.
5. Bake at 300°F (150°C) for 12-15 minutes.
6. Cool and fill with ganache or buttercream.

Chocolate Soufflé

Ingredients:

- 4 oz dark chocolate
- 2 tbsp butter
- 2 egg yolks
- 2 tbsp sugar
- 2 egg whites
- 1/4 tsp cream of tartar

Instructions:

1. Preheat oven to 375°F (190°C). Grease ramekins.
2. Melt chocolate and butter together. Stir in egg yolks.
3. Beat egg whites with sugar and cream of tartar until stiff.
4. Fold into chocolate mixture.
5. Pour into ramekins and bake for 15-18 minutes. Serve immediately.

Raspberry Almond Tart

Ingredients:

- 1 tart crust
- 1/2 cup almond flour
- 1/4 cup sugar
- 1/4 cup butter
- 1 egg
- 1/2 tsp vanilla extract
- 1 cup fresh raspberries

Instructions:

1. Preheat oven to 350°F (175°C).
2. Beat butter and sugar, then mix in almond flour, egg, and vanilla.
3. Spread into a tart crust and arrange raspberries on top.
4. Bake for 25-30 minutes until golden.

Baked Alaska

Ingredients:

- 1 small sponge cake
- 1 pint ice cream
- 3 egg whites
- 1/2 cup sugar

Instructions:

1. Place ice cream on sponge cake and freeze.
2. Whip egg whites and sugar until stiff peaks form.
3. Cover ice cream completely with meringue.
4. Broil for 1-2 minutes or use a torch to brown.

Matcha Green Tea Cheesecake

Ingredients:

- 1 1/2 cups graham cracker crumbs
- 1/4 cup butter, melted
- 16 oz cream cheese
- 3/4 cup sugar
- 2 eggs
- 1 tbsp matcha powder
- 1 tsp vanilla extract

Instructions:

1. Preheat oven to 325°F (160°C).
2. Mix crumbs and butter, press into a pan.
3. Beat cream cheese and sugar, add eggs, matcha, and vanilla.
4. Pour over crust and bake for 40-45 minutes.
5. Chill before serving.

Churros with Chocolate Dipping Sauce

Ingredients:

- 1 cup water
- 1/2 cup butter
- 1 cup flour
- 3 eggs
- 1/4 cup sugar
- 1 tsp cinnamon
- Oil for frying

Instructions:

1. Boil water and butter, then stir in flour until smooth.
2. Let cool, then mix in eggs one at a time.
3. Pipe into hot oil and fry until golden.
4. Roll in cinnamon sugar and serve with melted chocolate.

Sticky Toffee Pudding

Ingredients:

- 1 cup pitted dates, chopped
- 1 tsp baking soda
- 1 cup boiling water
- 1/2 cup unsalted butter, softened
- 3/4 cup brown sugar
- 2 eggs
- 1 1/4 cups all-purpose flour
- 1 1/2 tsp baking powder

Toffee Sauce:

- 1/2 cup butter
- 1 cup brown sugar
- 1/2 cup heavy cream

Instructions:

1. Preheat oven to 350°F (175°C). Grease ramekins.
2. Soak dates in boiling water with baking soda for 10 minutes.
3. Cream butter and sugar, add eggs, then mix in flour and baking powder.
4. Fold in the soaked dates.
5. Bake for 20-25 minutes.
6. For the sauce, melt butter, add sugar and cream, and simmer.
7. Pour warm sauce over puddings before serving.

Pistachio Baklava

Ingredients:

- 1 package phyllo dough
- 2 cups pistachios, finely chopped
- 1/2 cup sugar
- 1 cup melted butter

Syrup:

- 1 cup honey
- 1/2 cup sugar
- 1/2 cup water
- 1 tsp lemon juice

Instructions:

1. Preheat oven to 350°F (175°C).
2. Brush a baking pan with butter and layer phyllo sheets, brushing each with butter.
3. Add a layer of pistachios and sugar, then repeat layers.
4. Cut into diamond shapes and bake for 40 minutes.
5. Simmer syrup ingredients, then pour over hot baklava.
6. Cool before serving.

Vanilla Panna Cotta with Berry Compote

Ingredients:

- 2 cups heavy cream
- 1/2 cup sugar
- 1 tsp vanilla extract
- 1 1/2 tsp gelatin
- 3 tbsp water

Berry Compote:

- 1 cup mixed berries
- 2 tbsp sugar
- 1 tbsp lemon juice

Instructions:

1. Heat cream and sugar until warm. Add vanilla.
2. Bloom gelatin in water, then mix into cream.
3. Pour into molds and chill for 4 hours.
4. Simmer berries, sugar, and lemon juice for compote.
5. Serve panna cotta with berry compote.

Chocolate Éclairs

Ingredients:

- 1/2 cup butter
- 1 cup water
- 1 cup flour
- 4 eggs

Filling:

- 2 cups pastry cream or whipped cream

Chocolate Glaze:

- 1/2 cup chocolate chips
- 1/4 cup heavy cream

Instructions:

1. Preheat oven to 375°F (190°C).
2. Boil butter and water, then stir in flour. Cool slightly.
3. Beat in eggs one at a time until smooth.
4. Pipe onto a baking sheet and bake for 30 minutes.
5. Fill with pastry cream.
6. Melt chocolate and cream, then glaze éclairs.

Lemon Meringue Pie

Ingredients:

- 1 pre-baked pie crust

Lemon Filling:

- 1 cup sugar
- 1/4 cup cornstarch
- 1 1/2 cups water
- 3 egg yolks
- 1/2 cup lemon juice
- 2 tbsp butter

Meringue:

- 3 egg whites
- 1/4 cup sugar

Instructions:

1. Cook sugar, cornstarch, and water until thick.
2. Whisk in egg yolks, lemon juice, and butter.
3. Pour into the crust.
4. Whip egg whites and sugar into stiff peaks, then spread on pie.
5. Bake at 350°F (175°C) for 15 minutes.

Salted Caramel Brownies

Ingredients:

- 1 cup butter
- 1 cup chocolate chips
- 1 cup sugar
- 3 eggs
- 1 cup flour
- 1/2 tsp salt
- 1/2 cup caramel sauce
- 1/2 tsp sea salt flakes

Instructions:

1. Preheat oven to 350°F (175°C). Grease a pan.
2. Melt butter and chocolate, then mix in sugar, eggs, and flour.
3. Pour half the batter into the pan, drizzle caramel, then add the rest.
4. Bake for 30 minutes.
5. Sprinkle with sea salt before serving.

Almond Flour Chocolate Chip Cookies

Ingredients:

- 2 cups almond flour
- 1/2 cup butter
- 1/2 cup sugar
- 1 egg
- 1 tsp vanilla
- 1/2 tsp baking soda
- 1/2 cup chocolate chips

Instructions:

1. Preheat oven to 350°F (175°C).
2. Mix butter, sugar, egg, and vanilla.
3. Stir in almond flour and baking soda.
4. Fold in chocolate chips.
5. Scoop onto a baking sheet and bake for 12-15 minutes.

Opera Cake

Ingredients:

- 3/4 cup almond flour
- 3/4 cup powdered sugar
- 3 eggs
- 1/4 cup flour
- 2 egg whites
- 1 tbsp sugar
- 1 tbsp butter

Coffee Buttercream:

- 1/2 cup butter
- 1 cup powdered sugar
- 1 tbsp espresso

Chocolate Ganache:

- 1/2 cup chocolate
- 1/4 cup cream

Instructions:

1. Preheat oven to 375°F (190°C). Bake cake layers.
2. Make buttercream by beating butter, sugar, and espresso.
3. Make ganache by melting chocolate and cream.
4. Layer cake with buttercream and ganache.
5. Chill and serve.

Flourless Chocolate Torte

Ingredients:

- 8 oz dark chocolate
- 1/2 cup butter
- 3/4 cup sugar
- 3 eggs
- 1/2 cup cocoa powder

Instructions:

1. Preheat oven to 350°F (175°C). Grease a pan.
2. Melt chocolate and butter together.
3. Whisk in sugar, eggs, and cocoa powder.
4. Bake for 25 minutes. Cool before serving.

Tres Leches Cake

Ingredients:

- 1 cup flour
- 1 tsp baking powder
- 3 eggs
- 3/4 cup sugar
- 1/2 cup milk

Milk Mixture:

- 1 can evaporated milk
- 1 can sweetened condensed milk
- 1/2 cup heavy cream

Whipped Topping:

- 1 cup heavy cream
- 2 tbsp sugar

Instructions:

1. Preheat oven to 350°F (175°C). Grease a pan.
2. Beat eggs and sugar, then mix in flour, baking powder, and milk.
3. Bake for 25-30 minutes.
4. Mix milk mixture and pour over the cooled cake.
5. Whip cream and sugar, then spread on top.

Pumpkin Spice Roll Cake

Ingredients:

- 3/4 cup all-purpose flour
- 1/2 tsp baking powder
- 1/2 tsp baking soda
- 1 tsp cinnamon
- 1/2 tsp nutmeg
- 1/4 tsp salt
- 3 eggs
- 1 cup sugar
- 2/3 cup pumpkin purée
- 1 tsp vanilla extract

Filling:

- 8 oz cream cheese, softened
- 1 cup powdered sugar
- 1/4 cup butter, softened
- 1 tsp vanilla extract

Instructions:

1. Preheat oven to 375°F (190°C). Line a jelly roll pan with parchment paper.
2. Mix flour, baking powder, baking soda, cinnamon, nutmeg, and salt.
3. Beat eggs and sugar, then add pumpkin and vanilla. Mix in dry ingredients.
4. Spread onto the pan and bake for 12-15 minutes.
5. Immediately roll the cake in a towel and let cool.
6. Beat filling ingredients until smooth.
7. Unroll, spread filling, and roll back up. Chill before serving.

Pear and Almond Galette

Ingredients:

- 1 pre-made pie crust
- 3 ripe pears, sliced
- 1/4 cup sugar
- 1/2 tsp cinnamon
- 1/4 cup almond flour
- 1/4 cup sliced almonds
- 1 tbsp honey

Instructions:

1. Preheat oven to 375°F (190°C).
2. Roll out crust and sprinkle with almond flour.
3. Arrange pears in the center, leaving a border. Sprinkle with sugar and cinnamon.
4. Fold edges over pears. Brush with honey and sprinkle almonds on top.
5. Bake for 30-35 minutes.

Red Velvet Cupcakes with Cream Cheese Frosting

Ingredients:

- 1 1/4 cups flour
- 1 tbsp cocoa powder
- 1/2 tsp baking soda
- 1/2 tsp salt
- 1/2 cup butter
- 3/4 cup sugar
- 1 egg
- 1/2 cup buttermilk
- 1 tsp vanilla
- 1 tsp vinegar
- 1 tbsp red food coloring

Frosting:

- 8 oz cream cheese
- 1/2 cup butter
- 2 cups powdered sugar
- 1 tsp vanilla

Instructions:

1. Preheat oven to 350°F (175°C).
2. Whisk dry ingredients. Cream butter and sugar, add egg, then mix in wet ingredients.
3. Add dry ingredients and mix until smooth.
4. Bake for 18-20 minutes.
5. Beat frosting ingredients and pipe onto cooled cupcakes.

Black Forest Cake

Ingredients:

- 1 cup flour
- 1/3 cup cocoa powder
- 1 tsp baking powder
- 1/2 tsp baking soda
- 1/4 tsp salt
- 3/4 cup sugar
- 1/2 cup butter
- 2 eggs
- 1/2 cup milk

Cherry Filling:

- 1 can cherry pie filling
- 2 tbsp kirsch (optional)

Whipped Cream Frosting:

- 2 cups heavy cream
- 1/4 cup powdered sugar

Instructions:

1. Preheat oven to 350°F (175°C). Bake cake layers.
2. Mix cherry filling with kirsch.
3. Whip cream with sugar.
4. Assemble layers with cherry filling and whipped cream.
5. Garnish with chocolate shavings and cherries.

Strawberry Shortcake

Ingredients:

- 2 cups flour
- 1/4 cup sugar
- 1 tbsp baking powder
- 1/2 tsp salt
- 1/2 cup butter
- 2/3 cup milk

Filling:

- 2 cups sliced strawberries
- 1/4 cup sugar
- 1 cup whipped cream

Instructions:

1. Preheat oven to 400°F (200°C).
2. Mix dry ingredients, cut in butter, then stir in milk.
3. Shape into biscuits and bake for 15 minutes.
4. Macerate strawberries with sugar.
5. Slice biscuits, layer with strawberries and whipped cream.

Carrot Cake with Walnuts

Ingredients:

- 2 cups flour
- 2 tsp baking soda
- 1/2 tsp salt
- 2 tsp cinnamon
- 1 1/2 cups sugar
- 3 eggs
- 3/4 cup vegetable oil
- 2 cups grated carrots
- 1/2 cup walnuts

Frosting:

- 8 oz cream cheese
- 1/2 cup butter
- 2 cups powdered sugar

Instructions:

1. Preheat oven to 350°F (175°C). Grease cake pans.
2. Mix dry ingredients. Beat eggs, sugar, and oil, then add dry mix.
3. Fold in carrots and walnuts.
4. Bake for 30-35 minutes.
5. Beat frosting ingredients and spread over cooled cake.

Coconut Cream Pie

Ingredients:

- 1 pre-baked pie crust

Filling:

- 2 cups coconut milk
- 1/2 cup sugar
- 1/4 cup cornstarch
- 3 egg yolks
- 1/2 tsp vanilla
- 1 cup shredded coconut

Topping:

- 1 cup whipped cream
- 1/4 cup toasted coconut

Instructions:

1. Heat coconut milk and sugar.
2. Whisk cornstarch and yolks, then temper with hot milk.
3. Cook until thick, then stir in vanilla and coconut.
4. Pour into crust and chill.
5. Top with whipped cream and toasted coconut.

Apple Strudel

Ingredients:

- 1 sheet puff pastry
- 3 apples, sliced
- 1/4 cup sugar
- 1 tsp cinnamon
- 1/4 cup raisins
- 1/4 cup chopped nuts
- 1 egg (for egg wash)

Instructions:

1. Preheat oven to 375°F (190°C).
2. Toss apples, sugar, cinnamon, raisins, and nuts.
3. Roll out puff pastry, fill with apples, and roll up.
4. Brush with egg wash and bake for 30-35 minutes.

Classic Profiteroles

Ingredients:

- 1/2 cup butter
- 1 cup water
- 1 cup flour
- 4 eggs

Filling:

- 1 cup whipped cream or pastry cream

Chocolate Sauce:

- 1/2 cup chocolate
- 1/4 cup heavy cream

Instructions:

1. Preheat oven to 375°F (190°C).
2. Boil butter and water, then stir in flour.
3. Beat in eggs one at a time.
4. Pipe onto a baking sheet and bake for 25 minutes.
5. Fill with cream and top with chocolate sauce.

Chocolate-Covered Strawberries

Ingredients:

- 1 pint strawberries
- 1 cup chocolate chips
- 1 tsp coconut oil

Instructions:

1. Melt chocolate and coconut oil.
2. Dip strawberries, then place on parchment paper.
3. Chill until set.

Peanut Butter Mousse Cups

Ingredients:

- 1 cup heavy cream
- 1/2 cup creamy peanut butter
- 1/4 cup powdered sugar
- 1/2 tsp vanilla extract
- 1/2 cup crushed graham crackers (for the base)
- 1/4 cup melted chocolate (for topping)

Instructions:

1. Whip the heavy cream until soft peaks form.
2. In a separate bowl, mix peanut butter, powdered sugar, and vanilla.
3. Gently fold in the whipped cream.
4. Spoon crushed graham crackers into serving cups, then layer with peanut butter mousse.
5. Drizzle melted chocolate on top and chill for 1 hour before serving.

White Chocolate Raspberry Blondies

Ingredients:

- 1/2 cup butter, melted
- 1 cup brown sugar
- 1 egg
- 1 tsp vanilla
- 1 cup flour
- 1/2 tsp baking powder
- 1/4 tsp salt
- 1/2 cup white chocolate chips
- 1/2 cup fresh raspberries

Instructions:

1. Preheat oven to 350°F (175°C). Grease an 8-inch pan.
2. Mix butter and sugar, then beat in egg and vanilla.
3. Fold in dry ingredients, then mix in white chocolate chips and raspberries.
4. Pour into pan and bake for 25-30 minutes.
5. Let cool before slicing.

Mocha Tiramisu

Ingredients:

- 1 cup espresso, cooled
- 2 tbsp coffee liqueur (optional)
- 8 oz mascarpone cheese
- 1/2 cup heavy cream
- 1/4 cup sugar
- 1 tsp vanilla extract
- 12 ladyfingers
- 2 tbsp cocoa powder
- 1 oz dark chocolate, grated

Instructions:

1. Mix espresso and coffee liqueur.
2. Whip mascarpone, heavy cream, sugar, and vanilla until smooth.
3. Dip ladyfingers in espresso mixture and layer in a dish.
4. Spread mascarpone cream over ladyfingers, then repeat layers.
5. Dust with cocoa powder and grated chocolate.
6. Chill for 4 hours before serving.

Passion Fruit Tart

Ingredients:

- 1 pre-made tart crust

Filling:

- 1/2 cup passion fruit juice
- 1/4 cup lemon juice
- 3/4 cup sugar
- 3 eggs
- 1/2 cup butter, cubed

Instructions:

1. Whisk juice, sugar, and eggs over low heat until thickened.
2. Add butter cubes and stir until smooth.
3. Pour into the crust and refrigerate for 2 hours before serving.

Japanese Cotton Cheesecake

Ingredients:

- 8 oz cream cheese, softened
- 1/4 cup butter
- 1/2 cup milk
- 3 eggs, separated
- 1/2 cup sugar
- 1/2 cup flour
- 1 tbsp cornstarch
- 1/2 tsp vanilla
- 1/4 tsp cream of tartar

Instructions:

1. Preheat oven to 325°F (160°C). Grease a cake pan and line with parchment paper.
2. Melt cream cheese, butter, and milk together. Let cool.
3. Whisk in egg yolks, flour, cornstarch, and vanilla.
4. Beat egg whites and cream of tartar until soft peaks form. Gradually add sugar and whip to stiff peaks.
5. Fold into batter and pour into pan.
6. Bake in a water bath for 60 minutes. Let cool completely.

Chocolate-Dipped Biscotti

Ingredients:

- 2 cups flour
- 1 tsp baking powder
- 1/2 cup sugar
- 2 eggs
- 1 tsp vanilla
- 1/2 cup almonds, chopped
- 1/2 cup dark chocolate, melted

Instructions:

1. Preheat oven to 350°F (175°C).
2. Mix dry ingredients. Add eggs and vanilla to form a dough.
3. Fold in almonds and shape into logs.
4. Bake for 25 minutes, then slice into biscotti pieces.
5. Bake again for 10 minutes.
6. Dip in melted chocolate and let cool.

Mango Sticky Rice

Ingredients:

- 1 cup glutinous rice
- 1 cup coconut milk
- 1/4 cup sugar
- 1/4 tsp salt
- 1 ripe mango, sliced
- 1 tbsp sesame seeds

Instructions:

1. Cook glutinous rice according to package instructions.
2. Heat coconut milk, sugar, and salt. Pour over cooked rice and let sit for 15 minutes.
3. Serve with sliced mango and sprinkle with sesame seeds.

Homemade Baklava

Ingredients:

- 1 package phyllo dough
- 1 cup melted butter
- 2 cups walnuts, finely chopped
- 1/2 cup sugar
- 1 tsp cinnamon

Syrup:

- 1 cup honey
- 1/2 cup water
- 1/2 tsp lemon juice

Instructions:

1. Preheat oven to 350°F (175°C).
2. Mix walnuts, sugar, and cinnamon.
3. Layer phyllo sheets, brushing each with butter, and sprinkle nut mixture between layers.
4. Cut into diamonds and bake for 40 minutes.
5. Boil syrup ingredients and pour over hot baklava. Let soak.

Hazelnut Praline Cake

Ingredients:

- 1 1/2 cups flour
- 1/2 cup ground hazelnuts
- 1 tsp baking powder
- 1/2 tsp salt
- 1/2 cup butter
- 3/4 cup sugar
- 3 eggs
- 1/2 cup milk

Praline Topping:

- 1/2 cup sugar
- 1/4 cup chopped hazelnuts

Instructions:

1. Preheat oven to 350°F (175°C).
2. Cream butter and sugar, add eggs, then mix in dry ingredients and milk.
3. Pour into a cake pan and bake for 30-35 minutes.
4. Melt sugar in a pan until golden, then mix in hazelnuts.
5. Pour praline over cake before serving.

Dulce de Leche Flan

Ingredients:

- 1/2 cup sugar (for caramel)
- 1 cup dulce de leche
- 3 eggs
- 1 cup evaporated milk
- 1 cup whole milk
- 1 tsp vanilla

Instructions:

1. Preheat oven to 350°F (175°C).
2. Melt sugar in a pan to make caramel, then pour into a flan mold.
3. Blend dulce de leche, eggs, milks, and vanilla. Pour over caramel.
4. Bake in a water bath for 45 minutes.
5. Chill for 4 hours, then invert onto a plate.

Matcha Swiss Roll

Ingredients:

- 3 large eggs
- 1/2 cup sugar
- 1/4 cup flour
- 2 tbsp matcha powder
- 1/4 tsp baking powder
- 1/4 cup heavy cream
- 1/2 cup mascarpone cheese
- 1/4 cup powdered sugar

Instructions:

1. Preheat oven to 350°F (175°C) and line a 9x13-inch baking pan with parchment paper.
2. Beat eggs and sugar until fluffy.
3. Fold in flour, matcha powder, and baking powder.
4. Pour into the pan and bake for 12-15 minutes.
5. Let cool slightly, then roll the cake in parchment paper and let it cool completely.
6. Whip heavy cream, mascarpone, and powdered sugar.
7. Unroll the cake, spread the cream, and reroll the cake. Chill before serving.

Honey Lavender Ice Cream

Ingredients:

- 2 cups heavy cream
- 1 cup whole milk
- 1/2 cup honey
- 2 tbsp dried lavender flowers
- 1/4 tsp vanilla extract
- Pinch of salt

Instructions:

1. Heat milk, cream, and honey in a saucepan until warm, then add lavender.
2. Let steep for 15 minutes, then strain out lavender.
3. Whisk in vanilla and salt.
4. Chill the mixture, then churn in an ice cream maker according to manufacturer's instructions.
5. Freeze for a few hours before serving.

Chocolate Hazelnut Crepes

Ingredients:

- 1 cup flour
- 2 eggs
- 1 cup milk
- 2 tbsp melted butter
- 1/4 tsp vanilla extract
- 1/2 cup Nutella or chocolate hazelnut spread
- 1/4 cup chopped hazelnuts

Instructions:

1. Whisk together flour, eggs, milk, melted butter, and vanilla until smooth.
2. Heat a non-stick pan over medium heat and lightly grease it.
3. Pour batter to form thin crepes, cooking each for 1-2 minutes on each side.
4. Spread Nutella on each crepe and sprinkle with chopped hazelnuts.
5. Roll up the crepes and serve with extra chocolate drizzle.

Italian Cannoli

Ingredients:

- 2 cups ricotta cheese
- 1/2 cup powdered sugar
- 1/4 tsp vanilla extract
- 1/2 cup chocolate chips
- 12 cannoli shells
- Chopped pistachios (optional)

Instructions:

1. Drain ricotta cheese for several hours.
2. Mix ricotta, powdered sugar, and vanilla in a bowl.
3. Fold in chocolate chips.
4. Fill cannoli shells with the ricotta mixture and garnish with pistachios.

Bananas Foster

Ingredients:

- 2 bananas, sliced
- 2 tbsp butter
- 1/4 cup brown sugar
- 1/4 cup dark rum
- 1/4 tsp cinnamon
- 1/4 tsp vanilla extract
- Vanilla ice cream

Instructions:

1. Melt butter in a skillet over medium heat.
2. Stir in brown sugar, cinnamon, and vanilla.
3. Add sliced bananas and cook until tender.
4. Pour in the rum and carefully ignite (flambé).
5. Serve over vanilla ice cream.

Pecan Pie Bars

Ingredients:
Crust:

- 1 1/4 cups flour
- 1/4 cup powdered sugar
- 1/2 cup butter, cold and cubed

Filling:

- 1/2 cup light corn syrup
- 1/4 cup brown sugar
- 1/4 cup butter, melted
- 2 eggs
- 1 tsp vanilla extract
- 1 1/2 cups chopped pecans

Instructions:

1. Preheat oven to 350°F (175°C).
2. Mix crust ingredients and press into a baking dish. Bake for 12 minutes.
3. Whisk together filling ingredients, then pour over the baked crust.
4. Sprinkle with chopped pecans.
5. Bake for 25-30 minutes. Let cool and cut into bars.

Chocolate Espresso Mousse

Ingredients:

- 1 cup heavy cream
- 4 oz dark chocolate, chopped
- 2 tbsp espresso coffee
- 2 tbsp sugar
- 1 tsp vanilla extract

Instructions:

1. Melt chocolate and espresso together in a heatproof bowl.
2. Whip heavy cream and sugar until soft peaks form.
3. Fold whipped cream into the melted chocolate until smooth.
4. Chill for 2 hours before serving.

Rose Water Pistachio Cake

Ingredients:

- 1 cup flour
- 1/2 cup ground pistachios
- 1 tsp baking powder
- 1/2 cup sugar
- 1/4 cup butter, softened
- 2 eggs
- 1/4 cup milk
- 1 tsp rose water

Instructions:

1. Preheat oven to 350°F (175°C) and grease a cake pan.
2. Mix dry ingredients in one bowl and wet ingredients in another.
3. Combine and pour into the pan.
4. Bake for 25-30 minutes.
5. Let cool and drizzle with rose water syrup (optional).

Bourbon Bread Pudding

Ingredients:

- 3 cups cubed day-old bread
- 1 cup milk
- 1/2 cup cream
- 3 eggs
- 1/2 cup brown sugar
- 1/4 cup bourbon
- 1 tsp vanilla extract
- 1/2 tsp cinnamon
- 1/4 cup raisins

Instructions:

1. Preheat oven to 350°F (175°C).
2. Whisk together milk, cream, eggs, sugar, bourbon, vanilla, and cinnamon.
3. Pour over bread cubes and let sit for 10 minutes.
4. Stir in raisins and bake for 40-45 minutes until golden.

Homemade S'mores

Ingredients:

- Graham crackers
- Milk chocolate bars
- Marshmallows

Instructions:

1. Place a piece of chocolate on a graham cracker.
2. Toast a marshmallow over an open flame until golden and place on top of the chocolate.
3. Top with another graham cracker and serve immediately.